Believe

— IN —

MAGIC

LOM ART

Illustrated by
Claire Scully

Written and edited by
Susannah Bailey

Designed by
Derrian Bradder

Cover design by
Angie Allison

First published in Great Britain in 2020 by
LOM ART, an imprint of Michael O'Mara Books Limited,
9 Lion Yard, Tremadoc Road, London SW4 7NQ

 www.mombooks.com/lom
 Michael O'Mara Books
 @OMaraBooks
 @lomart.books

A CIP catalogue record for this book is available from the British Library.

ISBN: 978-1-912785-30-8

3 5 7 9 10 8 6 4

This book was printed in China.

FSC
www.fsc.org
MIX
Paper | Supporting
responsible forestry
FSC® C010256

This book belongs to

....

The crow often symbolizes a new phase
in someone's life. If a crow appears
to you, it may mean that it is time
to start a new chapter.

The crow can also be interpreted
as a symbol of life, magic, mystery,
intelligence, flexibility and destiny.
Some even believe it brings bad luck.

The Sun – giver of light and heat –
is nature's most powerful force.

Harvest festivals celebrate the
magic of the Sun, which allows
crops to grow and creatures to
be nourished by its warmth.

Touch is a magical gift. At the next opportunity, hold a person or object in your hands and close your eyes. Then take a breath, and appreciate the joy and stability that the power of touch has brought you.

The Wheel of Fortune tarot card depicts life in a constant state of flux. At times, when we experience good fortune, we are at the top of the wheel, whereas when things aren't going as well we might be nearer the bottom.

However, the wheel is always moving, and this card is a reminder to cherish the moments when fortune is on our side, and to take strength in the knowledge that times of hardship will not last forever.

WHEEL OF FORTUNE

The wolf is one of the most magnificent, and most feared, creatures in the animal kingdom. Sometimes associated with death and destruction, they are also fiercely loyal.

Wolves work as part of a pack and their teamwork helps them to predict situations and adapt to overcome them. By following their example, we too can connect with those around us and gain control over our lives.

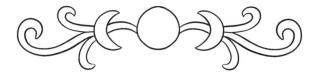

Herbs and flowers contain properties
to aid healing and self-care.

Lavender:
for purification, attraction
and restful sleep

Sage:
for cleansing, good luck
and driving out bad energy

Rosemary:
for strength, wisdom
and protection

The seasons are a stunning representation of change happening before our eyes. From blossoms blooming in spring to leaves falling golden in autumn, the natural world works in perfect, cyclical harmony, giving us the comforting knowledge that what is lost in winter is renewed in spring. This is Mother Earth at her most splendid and mesmerizing.

These triangles represent the four elements: air, earth, water and fire. They are integral to the ritual and magic of the world that surrounds us, and are connected to everything – from life and birth to destruction and death.

An unseen fifth element, that of the spirit, also exists. Present in the other four elements, it represents a sacred connection to the mystical part of the universe.

Owls have always been associated with wisdom. They sit still, observing the world around them before making any sudden movements. When they make a move, they do so silently and accurately.

The owl is a reminder to us all that it's better to plan our next steps with care and awareness, rather than rush hastily into the unknown.

Three earth signs make up part of the Zodiac. Those born under earth signs are wise, grounded and practical, although they can also be stubborn, with a tendency towards rigid thinking.

Capricorn:
ambitious, realistic, caring

Taurus:
patient, loyal, generous

Virgo:
organized, honest, dedicated

In ancient mythology, the phoenix was
a bird that set itself on fire and was
born again from its own ashes.

In modern times, the phoenix appearing
from the ashes symbolizes our ability to begin
again; despite challenging circumstances
we rise – stronger and more powerful
than we were before.

The Tree of Life is symbolic of how everything in the universe connects – from the roots of the trees, sustained by the soil, to the tips of the leaves, nourished by the light of the Sun. This energy, which we receive from all living things, creates a powerful cycle that unites us all in harmony.

The Triple Goddess symbol shows a waxing (growing) moon, followed by a full moon and then, finally, a waning (fading) moon. These depict three stages of womanhood – the Maiden, the Mother and the Crone – and yet the sign is also representative of all aspects of divine female power.

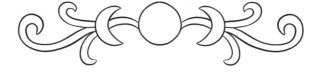

The hourglass represents and measures time.
Just as sand slips from the upper to the lower chamber
of the instrument, so do the minutes flow by.

The grains of sand may appear to be moving slowly,
but once they've fallen they cannot be retrieved. This is
a reminder that existence is fleeting, and we must
treasure the moments before they slip away.

Starting as tiny caterpillars that are enveloped
in cocoons until they finally emerge as beautiful
butterflies, these creatures symbolize
new beginnings and life cycles.

Their ultimate metamorphosis shows the power
of change, and the magnificence that can present
itself when one has patience and trust in the
natural processes that are all around us.

The Triquetra is an ancient symbol often found on runestones. It is used to represent the fundamental elements of earth, water and air, and when discovered on a rune can also afford protection to those that hold it sacred.

Traditionally, a wise woman is one with
a knowledge of herbs, healing, medicine and
other folklore. She often also has knowledge
of midwifery and divination.

A wise woman has a deep connection with the
natural world and her sacred knowledge has been
viewed with deep respect, and sometimes
suspicion, since ancient times.

Three fire signs make up part of the Zodiac.
Those born under fire signs are passionate
and dynamic, although they may also display
self-destructive tendencies.

Leo:
creative, sensitive, faithful

Aries:
strong, impulsive, charming

Sagittarius:
intellectual, adventurous, candid

Rituals, the ceremonies we perform to change something, are a key part of the practice of Wicca.

We can use them for healing, fertility, protection and banishing negative thoughts or influences from our minds and surroundings.

The High Priestess tarot card is representative of wisdom, mystery and sensuality. The crescent moon at her feet symbolizes her connection with the Moon's natural cycles and their link with the divine feminine.

The High Priestess appearing in a reading is a sign to remain calm and look for guidance, rather than jumping into action. The world's secrets will reveal themselves to those who wait.

HIGH PRIESTESS

A key is a symbol of freedom and liberation.
By opening a lock, you can choose to enter into
a new world, or to escape from the one behind you.

Keys also give you power and knowledge and, by
fitting perfectly into a lock, show that things will
always connect together if they are meant to be.

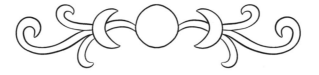

Ursa Major, meaning 'great bear', is a constellation in the Northern Hemisphere. It contains all seven stars that form the Big Dipper, one of the most recognizable landmarks of the dark sky.

On a clear night, look up to the Big Dipper and contemplate the beauty of the stars. Let the the magic of observing them light up the firmament around you.

Hecate's Wheel is the symbol of the ancient Greek
Moon goddess, Hecate, who rules over earth, sky
and sea and is associated with protection.

Hecate's Wheel is made up of a circle, inside of
which is a labyrinth, a common symbol of rebirth.

The spiral at the heart of the labyrinth
represents divine thought.

The snake has long been associated with transformation,
due to its ability to shed its skin. Wrapped around
a cracked mirror, a sign of bad luck, the snake is a
reminder to reflect upon who you once were and whether
you like and respect the person you have now become.

As the snake discarding its old skin shows us,
it is never too late for new beginnings.

There are eight phases of the Moon: new moon, waxing crescent, first quarter, waxing gibbous, full moon, waning gibbous, last quarter and waning crescent. These show the Moon's journey from a new, young goddess to one in her prime and, finally, to her fading in age. She is then born again as the cycle is renewed.

The phases of the Moon are highly significant. Each one has a different energy and they all hold a huge influence over our lives.

Ancient wisdom has been handed down through the pages of trusted books for centuries. Generations of Wicca practitioners can gain knowledge, insight and power from those who came before them. For this reason, books are an invaluable way of speaking to, and providing a connection with, our ancestors.

Bats often live in caves, enveloped in darkness
during the day before emerging into
the world each evening.

As nocturnal creatures, they can be
associated with black magic. However, when
dusk creeps in and hundreds of them flood
the sky at once, they can also be symbols of
rebirth and beginning anew.

Three water signs make up part of the Zodiac.
Those born under water signs are intuitive and sensitive,
although they also have a tendency to overthink things
and brood on them, which can be unhealthy.

Scorpio:
energetic, passionate, mysterious

Pisces:
romantic, nurturing, imaginative

Cancer:
sympathetic, persuasive, emotional

The harvest moon, the full moon closest to the autumn equinox, is often the brightest of the year. It is thought, therefore, that this is the most powerful time for spellwork, as the Moon goddess is at her most fertile.

The final harvest before winter arrives is also a reminder to take stock of where you are both physically and spiritually. It is a time to organize yourself in preparation for the long winter ahead.

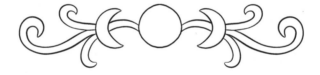

Spirit animals are guides who protect people as they undertake great journeys. They will often share characteristics with those they are safeguarding.

Birds are the perfect spirit animal to escort you on a journey of freedom; just as they fly high in the sky, so they encourage their charges to liberate themselves from the worries and troubles of earthly concerns.

The all-seeing eye is a symbol associated with knowledge and power. Often featuring in Christian iconography to show the omnipresence of God, the eye is also used in Wiccan rituals to ask for ultimate protection from the Sun goddess.

The Ace of Cups tarot card symbolizes
new beginnings and potential in relation
to love, happiness and creativity.

While the card is often associated with
romantic relationships, it can also represent
love in all areas of life, such as familial
love and love between friends.

ACE OF CUPS

Ravens, with their black plumage
and their menacing calls, are often
perceived as harbingers of bad fortune.

However, the Wiccan tradition recognizes the
raven as the most magical of birds. It is a divine
messenger that foretells the future and is symbolic
of both great mental clarity and spiritual energy.

Herbs have special powers to help in
the processes of healing and ritual.

Wise women use herb charts, such as the one opposite,
to decide which herbs to use at upcoming ceremonies.
They will glance at a chart and pick the plants that are
needed for a particular purpose, or simply choose
those that are calling to them to be selected.

SAGE

BASIL

ROSEMARY

THYME

BAY LAUREL

TARRAGON

MINT

OREGANO

PARSLEY

Formed over millions of years by fire,
wind and water, crystals have healing
powers gained from the sky and the earth.

They have different powers and it is important to find
crystals that speak to you personally. Hold them one at a
time in the palm of your hand and close your eyes – you'll
be able to feel which crystal your life force is drawn to.

The stag is a lonesome figure associated
with patience and strength, and represents
the spirit of the forest.

He will often stand at the threshold of the
wood, acting as a gatekeeper to the world
of spiritual enlightenment within.

The ancient apothecary contains a myriad of treasures – from natural wonders taken from the earth, such as herbs and crystals, to candles and oils made by skilled hands.

Step inside to discover a sacred sanctuary for those looking to expand their Wicca practice and hone their craft.

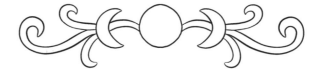

Sundials tell the time using the position of the Sun; as the Sun moves across the sky, the shadow created shows the hour of the day.

This invention emphasizes the power of the union between the human and natural worlds – by bringing nature's rhythms together with human ingenuity, great knowledge and harmony can be achieved.

It is an ancient tradition to throw coins into fountains. Water is our life force, and pure, drinkable water is something to cherish.

These glinting coins, therefore, represent our wish to stay healthy with purification, protection and healing.

Three air signs make up part of the Zodiac. Those born under air signs are communicative and curious, but can also quickly turn cold and unfeeling if they are crossed.

Aquarius:
artistic, truthful, confident

Gemini:
outgoing, expressive, independent

Libra:
idealistic, diplomatic, logical

Gates are often used to symbolize guarding. In a physical sense they may be used to keep something or someone in place, but metaphorically they may also refer to creating a wall of protection around yourself that is hard to relinquish.

Just as a locked gate becomes rusted over time, so a closed-off heart becomes harder to enter.

Consider opening your inner gate and letting in whatever feelings you are cloaking – once you unlock it, you may find it swings open easier than you anticipate.

Soaring above rivers and mountains, eagles are known for their grace and beauty, as well as their ability to swoop down on their prey with deadly precision. They represent power, freedom and self-discovery, encapsulated in the majesty of their wings as they dive through the sky.

Spiders are the ultimate symbols of patience.
They laboriously weave their beautiful webs and
then bide their time, waiting for their prey to find them.

Spiders teach us the vital lesson that the things we want
will often come to us if we lay a solid foundation for
them and simply have faith in a successful outcome.

Often found by foraging on the forest floor,
mushrooms grow in all shapes and sizes.

They have huge medicinal value and have long been
associated with healing. For this reason, mushrooms
can be useful ingredients to add to your rituals to
banish your ego and restore your inner balance.

When making your selection it is best to proceed with
caution, however, as amongst the beneficial fungi
the poisonous ones are almost always present.

The human skull is the starkest reminder that all of us must one day face our own mortality. It also shows us that when we cast away our earthly flesh humans are all the same as each other, no matter our status in this ephemeral world.

Flowers and plants growing here, however, also give us hope – our lives may be fleeting, but the wondrous cycle of nature will renew and repeat for eternity.

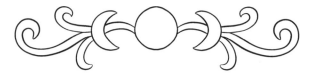

The flickering flame of the burning candle is the ultimate symbol of positivity. Creatures like the moth flock to it because, in the darkness, that tiny light can guide your way. So, when things seem bleak and unnavigable, look for a candle to illuminate your path and bring you safely to your next destination.

ARIES

LEO

SAGITTARIUS

TAURUS

VIRGO

CAPRICORN

GEMINI

LIBRA

AQUARIUS

CANCER

SCORPIO

PISCES